MyCoachExec

Thoughts to Guide You through a

Personal & Professional

Growth Journey

MYCOACHEXEC

outskirts
press

Outskirts Press, Inc.
http://www.outskirtspress.com

Paperback ISBN: 978-1-9772-3858-0
Hardback ISBN: 978-1-9772-3867-2

TABLE OF CONTENTS

PART 1
GROW YOURSELF

7 Thoughts to Guide You through Your
Personal and Professional Growth Journey

PART 2
GROW OTHERS

7 Thoughts to Help Others Grow Themselves

PART 3
GROW BUSINESSES

7 Thoughts to Guide you to Grow Businesses

To My Family,

Darren, for supporting me and encouraging me to live out my passion. Josh & Jake for inspiring me to want to keep growing and leave a legacy you can be proud of. Bonni & Kent, for always believing in me even when I didn't believe in myself. Bobbi, Henry, Phie, Sherri, & Carolyn for your love and fun through the years. Mom & Dad for being the foundation I know I can always come home to.

Love, #7

INTRODUCTION

MY GOAL WITH the book is to encourage you to grow yourself, grow others, and grow businesses through guided powerful questions, thoughts, stories, and situations. The goal is to inspire you to take action and create the results you want and make meaningful differences in your life, in others, and in your work. My personal mission for writing this book is to continue down a path of learning, growing, and reaching for new levels of understanding and knowledge each day so that my encouragement, my inspiration, and love for my kids, family, and friends will live on long after I leave this earth.

Personal and Professional growth is a path of development that transforms individuals to improve areas of their life and work they choose to focus on. Those areas may include their emotional and physical health, intellectual and spiritual growth, improved relationships, or their financial circumstances.

The desire to grow sometimes is triggered by an important life event that inspires you to concentrate on improving and investing in yourself by exploring within, where full potential and purpose lies. The results are that you will change and evolve into the person you are purposed to be, which will lead to a more meaningful, fulfilled life. This evolution will become apparent in your relationships, place of work, self-image, self-acceptance, as well as the world and everything else around you.

My purpose in this book is to encourage and inspire you; however, what lies within yourself, and learning how to tap into your own growth journey, is the very thing that will empower you to flourish. So, let's get started!

PART 1

GROW YOURSELF

7 Thoughts to Guide You through Your Personal and Professional Growth Journey

1

DESIGN YOUR DESTINATION

I HAVE GREAT respect for the past. In fact, I have to remind myself that I do not need to live in the past, but to accept it, all of it; the good of it, the bad, the magic, divine ordered steps, the heartaches and disappointments, love and love lost, the successes and failures, the people who passed through it, those who made an impact both positively and negatively, everyone and everything. I remind myself to reflect on the past in a way that I learn from it. Because if you know where you come from, you can certainly chart out your path to where you want to go.

What I discovered through all of my

experiences and decisions, is no matter what I have changed in my life, I am still right here inside myself. Through this discovery I recognize the responsibility I have is to myself. The responsibility to acknowledge and accept the person I really am, forgive myself for all the areas where I have failed, celebrate the great things that I have accomplished, and for the things that I need to recognize inside of me that no longer serves others or myself. My accountability is to lean into all ways that are loving, kind, and thoughtful, and, in turn, to become slower to anger, without judgment, full of grace—respectful, patient, encouraging, and considerate. It is difficult to stay in the flow of our soul purpose when life lessons come knocking at our door. When difficult circumstances arise—for example, if we experience a serious illness that impacts our very being both physically and mentally, when we find ourselves in a failing relationship, or a financial crisis that rocks our foundation—these events can change the path of our life over the course of years or in a moments time.

One of my areas of personal development is to let go of my past that binds me to certain beliefs that I allowed to settle in my core. These beliefs do not serve in a way that will allow me to flourish forward. For the sake of forward movement, personal growth, and understanding where I am heading next, it is my responsibility to close the chapters of the past that holds me back, only then will I start living my life that will propel me to my designed destination. My personal development leads to the now, giving me a new title of an "in the moment kind of girl," centered in the thought of flourishing in life to be the best I can be in the place I am in right now.

"My personal development leads to the now, giving me a new title of an in the moment kind of girl, centered in the thought of flourishing in life to be the best I can be in the place I am in right now."

Regardless of the roles of your life, your soul is seeking to find true purpose, your "Soul

Purpose." Your soul is always ready to guide you to a place of meaningful choices, decisions, and opportunities that will fulfill you, enlighten you, and sustain you. However, you must be ready to let go of your past and accept the responsibility of owning your self-development to move closer to your destiny. It is important to understand where you want to go. Recognize your inner thoughts which are preparing you to make changes that will be impactful in your life. Open up newness that will allow you to grow into your authentic purpose in this life and allow your individual greatness to be explored.

Again, if you know where you come from, you can certainly chart out your path forward to where you desire to go. Make peace with the things of your past that keep you bound, and hold on to the portions that will propel you forward, because that is when you can begin to design a new path to your destination. Where are you headed? What is your truest purpose in life? Are you on your right path?

2

ASSESS YOUR ATTITUDE

As INDIVIDUALS IN pursuit of a better version of ourselves, we are commissioned to cultivate our personal and professional lives in a manner that will set our thoughts and our hearts in the right perspective. It is important to feed your mind with thoughts of positivity, inspiration, and gratefulness so you can go as far as you can in life. What you think about yourself will morph into what you become. Therefore, think wisely, positive, goodness, healthy, genuine, smart, or better yet, genius; think purpose, passionate, happiness, gratefulness, think whatever it is that feeds your soul to the core of authenticity. I challenge you to think according to where you want to go in life, because your thoughts will lead you there.

"I challenge you to think according to where you want to go in life, because your thoughts will lead you there."

Several years ago, I began to meditate on how I wanted to grow professionally and where I wanted that growth to lead me. At the time I did not know how I would be able to accomplish what I had envisioned for myself, but nonetheless, I meditated on my growth mission. I wrote it down, added specifics around those thoughts and charted out actions to take and timeframes to get there. Most importantly, I believed in the process of setting my thoughts in a direction that would create energy and outcomes. I released the negative thoughts of whether or not it could even feasibly happen, and I allowed myself to focus on what I knew to be true, which was; where thoughts flow, energy goes. Therefore, I planned accordingly and had set my mind long before my vision for myself was even a viable option. I wanted to be ready for the opportunity when it presented itself. Sure enough, about 6 months after meditating continuously on my growth mission, the opportunity presented itself. I knew immediately this was my time, and I was certain in my heart that the opportunity was presenting itself to me because I had spent time in preparation, meditation, and positive thinking.

Opportunity + Preparedness = Success

It sounds hocus pocus, yet it is anything but. It takes focus, effort, sacrifice, dedication, mindfulness, and belief in the process and yourself. In order to continue to grow forward, stay prepared to capitalize on the opportunity when it presents itself. For me, this process seemed short for the time period during which I started meditating on this particular growth mission. However, the journey was well underway years in advance.

I had spent years making my way through college, while raising my sons, working a full-time job, and running a family household. I had worked through my self-doubt and fear of test taking and remained focused on my personal and professional growth and development. I vowed to be a life-long learner because the more that I learned, the more I realized just how much I didn't know. After all of the educational degrees and certifications that I've earned, and for all the business endeavors I've had the opportunity to be a part of, I stand amazed at how far I have come, yet humbled by the fact that there is so much more to learn. My learning journey has just begun, and though I will never be able to have all knowledge, I can always be in pursuit of more and of personal growth, as well.

Sometimes it is easy to sink back into thoughts that are negative and erode your progress in life. This can stem from various past experiences or even from current situations we live in. We believe that we are isolated by thinking all of the things that occurred in our lives are unique to us, such as growing up with any form of abuse—relationships, churches, illnesses that took joy from our life, regrets of choices in life that didn't turn out the way we thought it should, and so on.

Personally, I was raised in a religion that was led by a pedophile, who was referenced as the "man of the hour" meaning a profit or a man of God. He taught that the church would go through persecution in 1985, and Jesus was coming back for his "people" in 1992—that is, if we were not killed in the persecution beforehand. No surprise that this religion taught against furthering education, marrying anyone outside of that church and basically not having any type of real social life outside the confines of that church. I married at the age of barely 17, finished my Senior Year of High School as a married woman in a different town from where I was raised. I divorced 4 years later only to be ousted from the church I grew up in and viewed as a "tainted" woman at the age of 20. The choices I made at that critical time in my life were based on the teaching that the year I was to graduate High School, the persecution would take place. I wanted to experience life so I rushed it. I left my friends, family, and support system at a very young age. My parents didn't want me to get married that young, but as a 16-year-old teenage girl, I was adamant. They told me that I had to go counsel with the leader of our church to get permission. Part of me wanted him to say no, which I know now was my intuition, but instead he gave me his blessing to get married. It was not the outcome my parents were expecting, but the decision was made.

I was naïve, brainwashed, hurt, and confused. Like most victims, I found myself in another relationship only a few months after my divorce, this time out of my childhood religion. I was married again, for 22 years, had two children and managed through a relationship that was broken for many reasons, some of which I now recognize as my own issues. There was unresolved hurt swept under the rug, and other circumstances (that were not mine to own at all) led to the failure of my second marriage. I battled through years of cyclical chronic migraines that debilitated me for days, which led to depression and basically an unhappy life.

The point in giving a snapshot of some of my life experiences is to share that I too, like most of us on this earth, have experienced dysfunction and have had to overcome and push fiercely forward to come out better on the other side. After pausing to recognize what has already happened, the real question to ask regarding our past experience and dysfunction that shaped our minds and intellectual thinking in our young foundational years, is, how do you choose to live your life now? How are you going to stop focusing on what was a part of your life and start focusing your energy and thoughts on what you want in your life now? Harder said than done, but Let It Go, all of it, no matter what it is, because that is a gift that you can give to yourself, and quite honestly, those around you. When I say, "Let it Go," I mean the hurt, the nega- tivity and strong-holds, resentment, or what- ever your feelings may be that hold you back. If you cannot find some- thing to help you grow through the dysfunction and challenging experi- ences in life, you remain

"If you cannot find something to help you grow through the dysfunction and challenging experiences in life, you remain the victim."

the victim. Create a new life within, and move forward to a path that leads you to a growth journey unique to you. Assess your attitude, change your story, chart your future, and live the life you want to live.

3

GENERATE YOUR GOALS

SETTING GOALS IS a foundational practice of personal and professional development. As outlined in the first thought, "design your destination," it is important to set goals that will inspire you to head in the direction that you want to go. Write down your goals and fully embrace them, so they inspire you to go further in life and encourage you to believe you can reach them.

The real value of setting goals is for yourself, and the bravery to achieve them, not the recognition or kudos that you receive from others. The value comes when you go through the process of changing your life through your efforts of dedication, perseverance, and commitment to becoming the person you set out to be. If you choose to get my Grow Yourself Workbook, there is a guide that will help you align your passion to your work and values. It is important to know what you stand for, your core values, your principles, and your purpose in life, then to align it to the people, groups, or entities you want to serve. Once you align your goals around your personal mission, you can gain clarity as to why you are setting the goals in the first place.

I wrote a personal mission statement in 2010, which was: "My mission is to encourage, inspire, and love others to create an environment of peace and health for everyone that crosses my path in this life." In 2011, I added "including myself" at the end of that mission statement. This mission statement allowed me to get clear about the work that I did for a living, and the life that I was living personally, and, quite frankly, to motivate me to keep moving forward.

I have spent 27 years working in the

Healthcare Industry. The organization that I work for aligns with my personal mission through the focused effort on the care of the members' health at the heart of all of our business initiatives. In my own life, my personal mission statement was a powerful affirmation of this, because I had gone through some health challenges, that led to anxiety, depression, negative emotions, and lack of peace overall. In addition, my oldest son went through 11 years of having serious health issues that were misdiagnosed in the medical world and treated incorrectly. This led him into some extremely challenging experiences throughout his high-school and college years. I poured all of the energy I had within me to encourage, inspire, and love him so that our lives could exist in an environment of peace and health. For many years it was a challenge to find that balance because the circumstances were hard, and I struggled in numerous aspects of my life. However, after writing my mission statement, I visited it often to remind myself why I was doing what I was doing, to keep on track and follow through with the mission I set out to accomplish.

I will never forget the last time I went into the hospital with my son where he had experienced another serious cycle of illness. This was on the heels of him having a surgery in which we were told would cure him of his illness. That doctor was wrong, and still to this day I believe that malpractice was administered, but my son was so sick, my life was turned upside down, and I was struggling to fight through it all. I didn't have the time or the energy to fight the wrong that had already been done. I had to focus forward. We were desperate for a change that could bring peace and health. When you get desperate enough, when as a mother you go into "mama bear" mode, there is nothing that is going to keep any kind of force from stopping you until you have accomplished what you set out to do. In my case, at this particular time was finding a way to health for my son. What does this have to do with setting goals, you may ask? Everything. It's finding that passion to drive you to the aligned goals you've set out to accomplish. Sometimes the passion will come from pure desperation; other times it will come from pure joy.

So back to the story. As with every other cycle of sickness, after a day or two, my son would recover and appear to be perfectly normal and healthy. There he lay in the hospital bed, looking as if nothing was wrong, laughing and joking with the nurses. The nurse came in and said "you get to go home now." I had decided that we were not leaving until I understood what was taking place with my son's health. They had not been able to properly diagnose him, had put him through an unnecessary surgery to remove his gall bladder, ran the same multiple tests that they had run for years with no plan of action to get him healthy, and I knew we would be right back in the emergency room in a week or less. I had "set up shop" in the hospital room and was conducting my work there and had every intention of staying there however long it took for someone to tell me something different that we could do to get him healthy. Eight different doctors came in stating the same thing over and over. I kept asking for a specialist. I wanted to see every single test result, and I wanted it to be explained to me. I wasn't leaving until I could get answers. The last doctor came in and I asked him "If this was your son, what would you do?" That is when things began to happen, and it was the beginning of our road mapping toward a set of goals and a plan of action to get closer to a life of peace and health for my son.

Within a week, my son flew up to Cleveland Clinic, was seen by a Neurologist, and was properly diagnosed with having severe IBS (irritable bowel syndrome) and CVS, which is short for Cyclic Vomiting Syndrome, in essence a migraine within your stomach, which triggers a complete neurological event that takes place inside your body. While CVS is not curable, properly treated, a person can live a life that is so much more peaceful and healthier so that the cycle of these events is far less severe with the proper treatment.

I shared this story because it was my motivation behind my personal mission statement. It was a way for not only my son to live a more peaceful and healthy life; it was also an effort to create that same environment in my home that impacted our entire family. Once diagnosed, my son and the Neurologist set health goals, put action items in place to meet those goals, so that my son could pursue a path to health. It was a process to get there, and there are still times that it has to be re-evaluated in order to address the various recurring symptoms; yet they are on the right path to meet the goal of health, which in turn will bring more peace. My only regret in this situation is I wished I had pushed harder for answers sooner. The lesson learned in it for me is we all have power to speak up for ourselves and our loved ones. Regardless of what others are doing or saying, even if it is an expert doctor, if you know something isn't right, stand up, self-empower and have a voice. I said it once, but this is worth repeating: the real value of setting goals is for yourself and going through the process of changing your life through your efforts of dedication, perseverance, and commitment to becoming the person you set out to be.

> *The real value of setting goals is for yourself, and the bravery to achieve them, not the recognition or kudos that you receive from others. The value comes when you go through the process of changing your life through your efforts of dedication, perseverance, and commitment to becoming the person you set out to be.*

Everyone has something to inspire them enough to work toward self-generated goals that propel them forward and give them the desire to reach them. For me, it was knowing where I came from, fighting to work my way out of a childhood religion while still

feeling worthy of something more for myself and my family. It was becoming a mom,
being completely responsible for a precious
baby that grew up, faced challenges, severe
health challenges, during some of his prime
years of growing. It was in the joy that I saw
in my youngest son, knowing I never wanted him to lose the joy based on circumstances
that I could possibly help. It was in the recognition that I needed to further my education
and take ownership of my future. I knew that
what I didn't want in my life was at my door-
step. I knew where I came from, where I had
been, and where I was at that moment in my
life, were completely different from where my
designed destination would lead me. What is
inspiring you to set goals?

4

ACCELERATE YOUR ACTIONS

UNLIKE SETTING GOALS, action does not come from thoughts. Action comes from being prepared for the responsibility to own your path in life. It requires you to own your personal and professional development in order to move toward the opportunity of your highest potential of success.

In sharing a little snapshot of my life earlier, I mentioned that as part of the foundation of the religion I was brought up in, formal education was frowned upon and considered to be "of the world," rather than a means of growing and developing yourself and gaining knowledge. After going through my teenage marriage and divorce, and then remarrying and now with a two-year-old son, I knew I had to take action to improve my life for myself and my son. College was a daunting thought; however, with the encouragement and support of mentors, my parents, and the financial support from my employer through the tuition reimbursement program, I started the long journey of earning a Bachelor's Degree almost 9 years after I had graduated from High School. I worked a full-time job, took care of my family, and went to school evenings and weekends. My marriage was on the rocks, which led me to a separation, wherein my son and I packed up and moved back to my hometown to live with my parents. My son's father and I commuted for 2 years every other weekend, in an effort to repair the broken marriage, but I was adamant about staying with my parents and finishing up my degree before I would consider moving back.

During the time I was back with my parents, I used the opportunity to focus and take action on my goal to complete my Bachelor's Degree. I was able to transfer 36 credit hours over from the hours I had accumulated at the University of Louisville, and I set a goal to complete my degree within two years! I was focused and diligent in writing down every action item that needed to be complete for every single class. I had highlighters and lists that I would cross off each time I completed one action item that got me closer to my goal. Most nights I would fall asleep in my books after a full day in classes, working a side job of cleaning houses, spending time with my son who started kindergarten that year, and putting my health and fitness as a priority. By taking a full load every semester, summer classes, and even getting advisory board permission one semester to take 21 credits in one semester, I was able to complete my Bachelor's Degree in 2 years.

It is one thing to set goals and write down action plans to accomplish those goals, but it is a whole different level of commitment to accelerate those action plans and not let "life" get in the way. If you make it a priority, you will find the time. If you don't, it's only excuses.

Do you see how these thoughts are building upon each other? Designing your destination and knowing where you are headed, assessing your thoughts and attitude, setting your goals and taking action: these are all interrelated, which leads us to the next thought of releasing whatever you are resisting and understand what is stopping you now from moving forward.

5

RELEASE YOUR RESISTANCE

AFTER I FINISHED my Bachelor's Degree, my son and I moved back with his father and began to try and rebuild our relationship again as a family living under the same roof. I am not going to lie. This was not an easy transition for me, because I felt I had to explain why I was moving back and explain why I made the decision to give my marriage a second chance. I had a level of embarrassment and shame because all of our friends and family knew how far south our marriage had gone, down to the point of us drawing up divorce papers, and going through the steps of an ugly divorce, but never signing the papers. I know a lot of my friends reading this are most likely shaking their heads about now, but we made it through that time period, and we did have several good years afterwards, that led to having another son. I am very grateful for that time in my life, regardless of the ultimate later outcome of the dissolution of marriage.

After all I had been through to this point, another critical blow found its way to my life when I lost my job after the 9/11 attack on the U.S. It was the first time in my life, since the age of 13, that I had been "let go." I can't really tell you exactly why this particular incident was the one that took me to the lowest point that I had experienced in my life, but it did, and it shook me to the core. My life, my finances, and my health started spiraling downward. I felt isolated, and my relationship with my husband had already started slipping back into a patterned behavior that would lead us to another bad outcome. While this period of time was possibly the lowest point in my life, it is when I grew the most. Growing sometimes is painful because it can force you to face the truth, and the truth can cut deep if you allow things to pile up too long.

If I could go back to this particular time, I would have enjoyed my time off more. I wouldn't have worried so much about money or what people might be thinking of me – in fact I am certain they weren't thinking of me at all; it was all what I was trying to hang onto, without revealing my vulnerability and less than "perfect" side to my life. I would have enjoyed the summer with my 4-year-old, who started kindergarten that fall, and would have engaged in more conversations with my soon-to-be-high-school son. But I retreated into a version of myself that wasn't helping me grow by going back to thoughts of negativity, anxiety, and depression, which led to debilitating migraines. My younger son, Jake, so innocent, would come into my dark room and ask "Mommy, do you have a migraine?" He was so sweet at 4 years old that he would give me a towel for my head, whisper, and assure me that it would be okay.

Precious time was lost. There are many aspects to this period that I believe set the course for the next phase of my life, but I will not linger on any of the other events or stories in this time period, because I don't want what happened to be the focus of this section. Rather, I want us to learn from it so it can help all of us identify the time periods, lessons, gains and losses in our lives, to recognize that there may be some things we need help in uprooting to address the issues that were swept under the rug. There are many ways in which we detour away from fear of loss, fear of the unknown, embarrassment, and failure, exposing a side of us that we have tried to protect and not show to the rest of the world. When we do not fully address and work through critical issues that occur in our lives, go about our days as if nothing has hurt us, it will certainly show up later in our lives in some form or fashion. I believe that is where resistance occurs in our lives later to keep us from moving forward, especially if we feel we could be vulnerable to another embarrassing failure, financial despair, or exposure of a side of ourselves that makes us fear abandonment or disapproval from our loved ones.

Are there events in your life that may be causing you to resist moving forward? Do you feel as though you are stopping short of your fullest potential and success to protect yourself from future impact if you were to fall flat on your face in pursuit of your success? Some of the world's most successful individuals such as Thomas Edison, Albert Einstein, J.K. Rowling, Abraham Lincoln, Vincent Van Gogh, and Michael Jordan experienced multiple failures before they became successful. The key to their successes is, they never gave up. They had the determination, grit and drive to not give up on what they set out to accomplish. If you want to reach your goals, don't give up; keep moving forward. As the American writer, Albert Hubbard said: "There is no failure except in no longer trying." Get

motivated about your personal growth journey and when you experience failure or setbacks along the way to your success, accept it
and value it as another opportunity to learn
and grow towards your destination.

What is stopping you? Release the resistance, dig deep, expose it, deal with it, and
move forward to your fullest potential.

6

◆•◆

BE YOUR BRAVE SELF

◆•◆

HAVING WHAT YOU want in life and reaching success will take you down many paths, some great and some not so great. It requires many different things from you to step into your bravery. Like a vision forward, faith that you can make it, action to make it happen, and a lot of courage to take the necessary leaps. I can tell you that some of the scariest choices and decisions I have made to step out of my known comfort of misery (and into a life that would allow me out of the box that I had been put in for essentially all of my life), took some digging deep into the very depths of my heart and soul. I had to move forward courageously to change the course of my life forever.

It is easy to say "Be Brave, Be Courageous," but I will not say that it is easy to do it. There were long periods of times that I grieved over letting go of what once was, so that I could pursue and live the life ahead of me. I did not grieve because I regretted the decisions or choices throughout my life. I grieved because I had spent so many years and so much energy to create, hold onto, salvage, restore, and repair what was (or what I believed it to be), only to come to realize that I could no longer put energy into it *and* flourish forward into what I am destined to become. The major circumstances and changes in my life challenged me, and I had to make a decision to leave a part of my life and myself behind. This hurt me as well as those I loved.

When circumstances happen in our life, it can make us insecure, exposed, fearful, or vulnerable. But those exact life experiences can propel us forward, igniting us to do more with our lives than we ever thought we could. Those experiences can be the very thing that will either draw us backwards or strengthen us to move forward.

I have learned that if you hold on to the past, it is impossible to move forward with new life, vigor, and a clear sense of self. But, when you are able to re-alize that your past does not have to depict your future state, you can release the hurt, learn from it, release it, let it go and move fiercely forward.

Life will have ups and downs, but it will be your passion that will pull you through times of ambiguity. Do you have the courage to act outwardly to pursue a life that you were meant to live? Will you continue to talk about could've, would've, should've,

"When you are able to realize that your past does not have to depict your future state, you can release the hurt, learn from it, release it, let it go and move fiercely forward."

instead of stepping out into the unknown and treading toward the deeper meaning of your life? I encourage you to Be Brave. Your life depends on it.

7

CULTIVATE YOUR CELEBRATIONS

WHEN YOU EMBARK upon a mission of growing yourself, it will challenge you, sometimes bring you through some disarray, and it will definitely pull you out of your own place of comfort. The goals that you set have to be considered and intentionally inspire you toward your best character of being. You have to make a personal commitment to yourself to complete your goals and see them through fruition. A growth journey requires a lot from us and it is no small endeavor, so as you pursue and prosper through it, it is absolutely necessary to pause and celebrate all of your successes along the way, both big and small.

I had made a promise to myself when I lost my job after 9/11, I was going to go back and get my Master's Degree once I was able to start working again and to utilize the benefit of an organization that paid tuition reimbursement. While I was working on getting back into the workforce after being "let go," I began to focus on the steps that it would take to get my Master's. I lined up all my references, wrote my essay for entry into Business School, completed all necessary administrative work, so that when I got the job, I was ready to enroll in classes. That is exactly what happened. I have to tell you that my decision to get that Master's Degree was partially out of fear of not being able to stack up against the competition in the marketplace if I was ever to lose my job again. I guess it was a move of protection on my part, but in the process of that insecurity, I was able to propel forward, use that energy to focus on something positive, and make strides toward growing myself personally and professionally. I worked like a machine, and I sacrificed my health, and time with my children to go to school on weekends and nights again in order to try and build a better future for them. Acting out of fear or any other negative feeling can often cloud your thoughts and cause imbalance in your life. While it is great that I completed my Master's degree while working full time, the journey was relentless and the price was high.

My advice to all of you on a growth journey is: approach your goals in a manner that will still allow you to enjoy your life, your loved ones, or children while they are young, to work on the areas of your life that are most important, and not lose sight of celebrating along the way. It cannot be "no work and all play," but it also cannot be "all work and no play." This is a lesson played out in so many cases in our society and in individuals who devote their very soul in lopsided proportion to one aspect of their life. The fact is, when that time is gone, it is gone. We only have right now. It is never too late to start a practice of being mindful of the balance in your life.

Be thoughtful and intentional about your growth journey, and recognize that it takes time. Give yourself grace and understand that it's not a single step but a whole journey filled with different obstacles and opportunities. Remember to keep a balance in your life by understanding what is important to you, why you are doing the things that you are doing, and by weighing all costs to your growth journey. To attain ultimate growth both personally and professionally, you have to overcome the obstacles

"Give yourself grace and understand that it's not a single step but a whole journey filled with different obstacles and opportunities."

one at a time and then be prepared for the opportunities that are presented to you. Don't forget to celebrate life to the fullest along the way. Schedule your celebrations; be just as intentional about celebrating as you are with your goal setting and action planning.

One of my favorite party songs is "Celebration" by Kool & The Gang. Take a moment, yes, you, take a moment, turn that song on and dance it out. Celebrate "good times and your laughter too," and have yourself a little celebration. What are you celebrating today? Come on, let's get this celebration started.

PART 2

GROW OTHERS

7 Thoughts to Help Others Grow Themselves

As a life-long learner, I have spent many years seeking higher education, focusing in the fields of Business Communications, Psychology, Business Management, Leadership, and Executive and Professional Coaching. In all of these areas of concentration, people are at the very center. When helping others to grow themselves, the first step is to build connections. Through the evolution of time, if we devote ourselves to helping others grow, we ourselves will continue to transform, grow, and evolve.

1

UNDERSTAND UNIQUENESS

EACH AND EVERY person has their own story to tell, and regardless of any similarities to others, it is still true that each person is uniquely designed and poised to share what they have to offer in this life. It is through their journey, their eyes, that they are able tell their story. We are living in times where the very essence of division in our country is based on the differences among ourselves and others. It

"It is critical that we start seeking to understand one another, understand everyone's uniqueness, and ultimately the value each person can share with the world."

is critical that we start seeking to understand one another, understand everyone's uniqueness, and ultimately the value each person can share with the world. As leaders, mentors, and coaches, our role in helping others grow is first to seek to understand and then to help others get clear on who they really are and what direction they want to go in their life.

Recently I was coaching a young professional who was looking to improve his leadership skills so that he could be respected and considered a valuable asset among his peers, clients, and leaders in his organization. I perceived during the coaching session that he was referring to how his leaders were forcing him to fit inside a parameter that took him far away from who he was as an individual, his uniqueness, his own greatness. We discussed how it made him feel further away from the passion he once had about his career, and instead he was now operating in a manner that separated him from who he was authentically. Though he was successful in his work and with his clients, the organization was shifting processes that would change the course of how they operated the day-to-day business. This in turn forced the young executive to identify how he would be able to adapt to this change, while not losing his uniqueness. After setting a few key actions for himself and acting on them, he was able to recognize that he could navigate through the new processes and change the way in which he operated without losing his ability to continue to be his unique self that his peers and clients enjoyed and benefitted from. I reflect on my own uniqueness. I did not have the traditional upbringing however, I know that my own unique journey brings a different approach, perspective, and value to the work that I do, the people I serve, and the relationships I have cultivated through the years.

Part of helping others grow is to help them recognize that their uniqueness is their strength and to use that strength to propel them to new heights.

What are your strengths? How are you leveraging your uniqueness to take you to your next growth level? What do you love most about your uniqueness?

2

ENCOURAGE EMPOWERMENT

WHEN GROWING OTHERS and developing leaders, as a Professional Executive Coach, I find it important to foster an environment that encourages empowerment. The highest calling in leadership is focusing on growth and development concentrating on empowerment with the right people. This act of intention helps with focusing on all types of people and how coaches have to approach guidance to their development. Self-awareness is the first step to growth and development. As leaders, we can never assume people will come naturally to having self-awareness.

In many cases self-limiting beliefs are deep-rooted, and can take time and work to be weeded out of the thinking process. Limiting beliefs can have a tremendous influence on your life and how you make decisions for yourself. However, one thought to help guide you away from your limiting beliefs is to practice in the now, be present in the moment, and gravitate to your new, positive mindset and belief system.

"Limiting beliefs can have a tremendous influence on your life and how you make decisions for yourself."

A former client of mine had been working for a company for several years, had made his way through college, and was aspiring to land in an executive position. He had been able to move up in the organization but was held back in his salary because he had started at such a low amount to begin his career, and his company policy allowed only so much of a percentage of increase, which resulted in him being paid almost half the salary as his peers in the same role.

We discussed that when he was growing

up, the money topic in his home and with his parents was kept very private, and asking about money was off-limits. This created a narrow belief about money that was deep-rooted and that had to be worked out of his thinking process in order to create a space where he felt comfortable moving forward to have a conversation with his leader. We established a plan together, and he was able to act upon his plan, have a money conversation with his leader, articulate why he deserved a raise, and was finally able to get beyond his limited belief about money in order to ask for the amount of raise he expected to receive. The action steps he took felt like a huge risk to him, but once he felt empowered to act and follow through, he found that the freedom he got from that exercise far outweighed the raise that he did end up getting. Since that time, he has excelled in his career and has a much stronger sense of empowerment by virtue of having gone through the process of overcoming his deep-rooted limiting beliefs, and by being encouraged to take the steps needed to move forward.

Your thoughts can transform your life. It is important to re-frame your negative thoughts about yourself, your life, and to have critical conversations so that you too can move forward. Do you have any limiting beliefs that hold you back? What is one step you can take to empower you to tear down those beliefs that are limiting you and keeping you from living your best life? Write it down, take action, and be set free.

3

VALIDATE VALUE WITHIN

THERE ARE MANY times that we throw away what has been broken in our lives, viewing it as a failure or invaluable, but every single life lesson, including the brokenness, brings some value that we can grow from. The key is to recognize the lesson in it.

I am reminded of a Japanese art tradition that is called Kintsugi, which has been described by some as the art of precious scars. Kintsugi is the process in which the artist uses liquid gold to repair valuable broken objects such as family heirlooms, like a grandmother's bowl or vase, not just to fix the item, but to bring more value once the fragments have been bonded back together with the liquid gold. This art technique brings uniqueness to every single piece of Kintsugi art. After the break, there is new life, and a specific uniqueness and enhanced value because of the process of being put back together as a whole.

Like Kintsugi artists, we are able to create true and unique growth paths that reflect our own story and beauty, beauty that will come from the experiences that crack and break us but cannot keep us broken. When we are able to see the beauty in our brokenness and see the scars that are left behind as liquid gold, we can then begin to recognize the value within.

I love how the Kintsugi art technique can mirror our life experiences. It suggests that when we have brokenness in our lives, it doesn't mean we no longer have value, quite the opposite. It means we have fortitude to go through the brokenness and come out on the other side, more cultured, individually valuable by the authenticity of our imperfections.

As I mentioned earlier, the religion I grew

up in did not allow for us to have relationships outside of the church. As I reflect back, it
was really designed to keep a clear separation
between those inside and outside of that religion. The more involved you were as a faith-
ful follower, the more conditioned you were
toward the church. Every part of life becomes
centered around it. It becomes your all, your
family, friend circle, and complete community
source. Removing yourself from this type of
environment after years of being engulfed or
born into it, is difficult, and sometimes feels
impossible. It can be frightening and isolating,
but I personally began removing myself from
the church after my divorce from my high
school marriage in 1988. I did experience iso-
lation, not because some of my church friends
did not reach out to me, but because I was
no longer accepted in that circle. I had made
a decision for myself that was "worldly" in
their minds. The church was a big part of my
identity. At this time in my life, the church
was still oblivious to the leader's pedophiliac

behavior, and he was still very much in leadership and power. Because of my upbringing, being taught to respect the leader, holding him in high regard, along with my deep affiliation with the church, I had a need to receive the approval or blessing from the leader after my divorce.

I mentioned earlier the brainwashing I experienced because it involved the loss of my own sense of power, the feeling of being trapped, unable to leave or go against the teachings in fear that something awful may happen because of my perceived "rebellion."

I went to have the discussion with the leader in hopes of receiving some sort of blessing so I could move forward in peace. That meeting was quite the opposite of what I was hoping for. He berated me, told me how horrible of a person I was, questioned my character, told me I would fail, blamed my mother because she was the one who came and picked me up and moved me back to my parents' home. He also made some terrible accusations toward one of my 5 sisters, one who had experienced physical and mental abuse in her church marriage. At the end of the meeting, in true manipulative fashion, he prayed for me and ordered me to go back to the marriage. This is the same church leader who told one of my friends that she lost her baby because of her rebellion. Even writing this down, all these years later, disgusts me, but it is snapshot of the brokenness that I experienced in my life, along with the numerous experiences that my friends and family went through in their lives.

Whatever your story is, wherever your life journey has taken you, whatever brokenness that you have experienced, the Kintsugi art analogy can encourage and inspire you to look at your life, the traumatic events or negative experiences, and reframe them from a positive point of view. As the Artisan of your own life, you have the opportunity to take the experiences of the brokenness, build it back together through the wisdom and knowledge you gained from the events, and bond those pieces to bring it back into wholeness. Call it the art of life, revealing the precious scars that come only from the uniqueness of your life story and experiences, bringing value only you can offer to others.

I will tell you that the scars left behind in my life have made me a stronger person. The brokenness has propelled me forward and has driven me to keep moving forward no matter what. It is in the peace that I feel to give forgiveness and grace to those who have been pillagers in my life. When I began my work for MyCoachExec, I started self-doubting. My thoughts started eroding my excitement about my work because my thinking was that I couldn't possibly reach my audience with words that would challenge, encourage, and inspire them. At first, I doubted that sharing some of my life, the dysfunction and broken-ness, would convey a message that would res-onate with others. Yet I took my own advice and continued to move forward with sharing parts of my life, my lessons, and knowledge in the way that only I can in this world. When you are able to open yourself to others in a way that is vulnerable and authentic, you will be able to uniquely share the value you have within yourself. Recognizing your own value within will open your eyes to see the value in others. My goal is to share my experiences so that, in turn, you may be enlightened on your own growth journey that will help you identify your value through vari-

"Recognizing your own value within will open your eyes to see the value in others."

ous thoughts, processes, and your own unique story. What areas of your life have you had to use liquid gold to put yourself back together? How did you grow from it? What value do you see in those areas of your life that challenged you, left scars, broke you?

4

CHASE CURIOSITY

WHEN I HEAR the word curiosity, I always think of the phrase, "Curiosity killed the cat." Yet in the realm of personal growth and growing others, curiosity is essential. Individuals who are curious believe they can learn, grow, and change. They understand that knowledge, understanding, and wisdom doesn't fall in their lap but that it is up to them to seek out for themselves. The best way to chase curiosity is to commit to learning something new each day or to experience something different: trying different foods, exercises, different routes to work or home, or simply meeting new people and learning something interesting about them. You must look at each day as an opportunity for curiosity that will lead to learning, being open to new thoughts, paths, and opportunities to expand your thinking.

As crazy as it may seem after all I have been through, I allowed myself to be curious about love again. I reconnected with Darren after 30 years since the last I had seen him. My sister lived in his home town and they ran into each other one day in which their conversations led us towards one another. I was scared of forward movement in this area of my life, but in time that fear turned into faith. Though the scars of my past are still visible, the value within the relationship I have with Darren has opened a complete authentic view of myself, into the areas that I wasn't able to see before. I am grateful for the curiosity about one another evolving into something more meaningful. Our personal and adventurous growth journey together has just begun.

A couple of years ago, Darren and I visited one of our favorite places to retreat to in

Sedona, Arizona. We had a long weekend there and had a few adventures planned. The last morning, we were there, Darren wanted to go out early for a hike before we had to pack up and head towards Phoenix to fly home. I was less enthusiastic about the idea of getting out the door at 5 a.m. to go hike for miles up-hill, but Darren was persistent. I grudgingly followed behind him in silence for the first 20 minutes of the hike, but the further up we got, the beauty in sight became breathtaking. The scenery jolted me out of my morning grumpi-ness over having to get out of my warm bed. I recognized that this adventure was something I had never seen before, never experienced at this level, and should therefore value the beauty that was all around me. After getting my blood flowing and my heart rate up, my eyes opened a little more. I was able to see the sun rising over the mountains, and, as a spe-cial treat, as if ordered by God, on the horizon, we experienced a multitude of hot air balloons coming over the red rocks, and I stood in pure awe of beauty and excitement. We took time to stand still in that moment, to take in the beauty, and appreciate where we were in the history of time.

I thought of my mentor and friend Helen, whom I used to work for when she was in charge of overseeing the Kentucky Derby Hot Air Balloon Race—and the memories we made being a part of that together for several years. I took pictures and sent them to her letting her know that I was thinking of her. A year later, she lost her life to cancer, but her memory will live on in the moments we had together and in that moment on the Sedona hike. She was not with me physically that trip, but she was in my thoughts and heart. In order to keep a mindset of curiosity, you have to remain focused on learn-ing, seek out different

"In order to keep a mindset of curiousity, you have to remain focused on learning, seek out different opportunities that will lead you to something you have never experienced, heard, or seen before."

opportunities that will lead you to something you have never experienced, heard, or seen before. I am grateful to Darren for persisting on the hike as a last adventure on that trip because it is a memory I will always have.

At the end of the day, reflect on what you learned, write it down if you have to, and recall your experience. Recall what you thought of, who you thought of, how you acted on those thoughts. If we all approach life this way it will keep us moving forward, eagerly anticipating our adventures the next day, and it will stimulate and challenge our minds to think more creatively. Stay curious, my friends, as it will lead you out of your mundane routine into a new adventure that will make you excited to get up in the morning to explore what is new for you that day. How will you chase curiosity in your life today? What excites you about living a life of curiosity? How will this manifest itself in your life?

5

ORGANIZING FOR OUTCOMES

ONE OF MY favorite authors is Marie Kondo, a Japanese organizing consultant who "sparked" a decluttering movement with her unique approach to decluttering. In the entryway of my home, you will find her lovely little book, Spark Joy, an illustrated master class on the art of organizing and tidying up, on the entry table, along with my heirloom vase that was my great-grandmother's my parents gave me for my birthday this year, and a picture of my beautiful mom when she was nearly 16 years old. These items give me great joy. Marie's approach essentially has two parts. As I would explain it, first, you gather everything that you own, ask yourself if it sparks joy, and if it doesn't, you thank it for its service to you and then get rid of it. Second, once you have gone through this process and you are left with only the things that give you joy, you start placing those items in a designated, accessible and visible place.

When it comes to my life, relationships, and businesses, I find great joy in organizing and seeing the results from this work. Similar to our physical surroundings, our growth journey will require us to take inventory of where we are, where we are going, and how we are going to get there. When coaching others, it is important to help clients recognize where they want to reorganize their path and determine their desired outcome. Once that is established, they will need to commit to a set of guiding principles for their personal and professional growth that will set the foundation to guide them through to their destination. By organizing this framework early in their growth journey, clients will be able to eliminate dependencies holding them back and concentrate on clearly defining which actions to take them toward the growth path that will lead them to a desired outcome that gives them joy.

I appreciate how the decluttering method of Marie Kondo takes inventory of everything in your house and starts the process of ridding of things that no longer serve you. The beauty lies in incorporating the gratitude toward that item before letting it go. Similar to our earlier topic of Be Your Brave Self, we have learned that if you hold onto the past, it is impossible to move forward with new life, vigor, and a clear sense of self. It's important to have gratitude for the things that showed up in your life, made an impact for a season but now no longer has purpose. Everything had a purpose at one time: for example, a piece of clothing that was bought and worn to a meaningful event where you made memories and celebrated life; it no longer fits you today yet years later still hangs in your closet. For me, I recall the multitude of t-shirts I held onto for years that commemorated a certain event, or years of my son's baseball or golf teams, or a favorite sleeping shirt. I had intended to use them to make a quilt or blanket, but never got around to making that happen. I think that we are all guilty in some fashion of hanging onto clutter physically and mentally. Use that as a metaphor for all the things you have piled up, cluttered your mind, heart, life with, the things that no longer serve their purpose. Realize that your past is not your future, give gratitude toward the lessons, joy, or meaning that it once gave you, then release it, let it go and move fiercely forward.

The best part of decluttering is how you feel afterwards. The reward is the clear spaces, the clarity, and purposeful placement of everything around you. This gives way for a new approach of thinking, learning, and growing. In your growth journey be prepared to declutter the things that you need to purge from your life. Decluttering isn't always about physical things. It can be emotional, habitual, and re-lational. Take inventory of clutter in your life, and know that when you recognize what has to be cleared out you are better equipped to organize the outcomes of your life. Write down all of the things that come to mind that you are holding onto. Let this be the beginning of setting up your framework to organize yourself for the joyful outcomes you desire. What brings you joy? Do you have clutter that you can remove from your life?

6

Purposeful Potential

PRIOR TO **COVID** shutdown, my work life encompassed a tremendous amount of travel around the United States, sometimes in multiple cities within a 24-hour period and multiple meetings with different clients. The workload and travel were intense but rewarding. There are always going to be pros and cons to both domestic and professional situations, but there are times when circumstances have a way of interrupting the flow and putting us on a different course.

We are now 10 months into COVID, workdays are longer via phone, emails, and virtual meetings, however, the travel has been suspended changing the way that I go about my life. During this lock-down, I have reflected on what I have prioritized and where I need to refocus some of my attention. During my reflection, I recognize that I had drifted into the mindset of "not enough." Meaning, excuses, really. I often hear from myself and from close friends that there isn't enough; time, energy, money, stuff, love, happiness, fun, food, space, or _____ [you fill in the blank]. These limitations that we put on ourselves cause us to operate in the mindset of lack. These might include negative thoughts about ourselves such as I am not thin, strong, smart, accredited, supported enough, etc., which brings us into a cycle of having a chronic feeling of inadequacy. Therefore, we seek out the next diet, start a new workout regime, or the next course, or the next relationship, and so on. We have lived this hurried life in pursuit of more. In doing so, we have decided that more is better, which grows into a programmed way of living in an attempt to justify what we haven't accomplished. This kind of thinking can take us off course of living a life of genuine fulfillment.

Purposeful potential is the very essence of taking what we do have and stretching it, instead of always being in a hurry chasing whatever it is we are chasing more of. The challenge of purposeful potential is to change the story of the perspective of lack because we can do more with what we already have. Just as we have learned to adapt to the new COVID environment, we can learn to use our resources differently. In reflection, I find it interesting that we get caught up in a world of always pursing more with the feeling of not having enough, but we are burdened by so much excess and clutter. As mentioned previously, clutter can be defined as physical clutter but also as mental and emotional clutter.

I shared earlier that when I was let go from my job after 9/11, it was one of the most challenging times of my life, but I also mentioned that it was a period of time when I grew as an individual. The environment that I found myself in forced me to take a look around and to use our resources differently, to stretch the things that were in our possession.

I talked with my oldest son about that particular time, and he recalls, as an example, having spaghetti for dinner often. What he didn't realize was it was out of necessity rather than choice. He didn't know the difference, and that was what mattered to me. I also took that time to evaluate the misuse of money that was flowing in and out of the household. There is something very cleansing about taking inventory of expenses that are excessive or unnecessary and cutting them completely out of your spending. Too often in our hurried lives we are not paying attention to what is going out and how quickly spending on any particular area can get excessive or out of hand. That is when excess builds up, yet we are so hurried in the pursuit of chasing the next thing of more. When you are forced into a scenario, it may be uncomfortable, but valuable lessons can be learned from it as well. Once you experience hardship, the lesson learned from it can be applied to other experiences that put you into uncomfortable environments.

As leaders, mentors, and coaches, we must ask our clients questions. How can they do more with what they already have? What areas can be inventoried, sold, or cleared out of their life? How can they get clear on where life is hurried and the destination they are hurrying to? What on the list of to-dos are critical in nature? If you were able to rid yourself of unnecessary events, spending, and time, what would you fill it with? Where is the purposeful potential in your life? What does it look like to you?

7

SERVE SELFLESSLY

ACTS OF SERVICE are a form of kindness and giving. I have shared my thought with people close to me that it is greater to give than to receive. Though it may sound like a cliché, I say it because when you are able to give, you are blessed yourself, but you also can bless others. During the timeframe that I was out of work, Christmas that year was very hard for us financially. While I had friends and family who offered help, I held guilt of some sort, and I just could not bring myself to accept it. I made a trip to Walmart where I had put a few things on layaway for the kids, which included the one item that my 4-year-old requested from

Santa: "Hulk Hands." It was going to be his big gift that year, by which I mean the cost was somewhere near $15.00. As I learned that I was a couple days late picking up my layaway and my items were put back and possibly sold, I went into sheer panic that I would not be able to get the highly sought-after Hulk Hands only a couple of days before Christmas. I frantically asked the Walmart associate to show me where they were, and as we reached the aisle, as I'd feared, there were no Hulk Hands to be found. I must have gone into complete meltdown, because one of the Walmart associates who saw me immediately stopped what he was working on, climbed down the ladder he was on, just to engage me and try to understand my dilemma.

When I shared that I was late picking up the layaway and the only thing I really needed was the Hulk Hands, he immediately went in the back and told me to sit on a bench until he returned. I could hear him in the back rallying all the workers in the back where the layaway items had been put back in bins that were piled high. They rummaged through them until they were able to find the pair of Hulk Hands, along with the list of items that I had on layaway. I was in such relief when he came out with the items I broke down in tears, but that was not the end of his selfless service. He asked me to go shopping and get whatever I needed and said he was going to override the cost. I was so embarrassed and just grateful for the Hulk Hands that I declined anything else he was offering, but he went to the register and checked me out himself with no cost to me for the remainder of the items that I had put back on layaway that year. He may have recognized my distraught state, but he did not have to go out of his way that day for me. I am forever grateful and will never forget how he made me feel and the difference he made for my kids Christmas.

When people have a service mindset, it will have a ripple effect in the networks and communities they serve. Studies have shown that when people witness individuals serving others, encouraging them, teaching them, they are inspired themselves to do the same. The "paying it forward" initiative can expand deep into other networks of individuals who will serve others and help others. Years later, I find myself in a relationship with Darren, who has participated in the Toys for Tots with the USMC League for many years. Toys for Tots is a Top-Rated Charity whose mission is to provide toys, books, and other gifts to less fortunate children. I too have participated many years in this same charity, along with Angel Tree, and random families whom I learn need help through financially difficult times. It is a reminder of where I have been, the impact that one person can make by selflessly serving others.

Individuals who serve have several practices that genuinely help others. They practice giving full attention and presence in whatever environment they find themselves. Their own agenda is put on hold for that moment, which allows for more awareness of others' needs. They listen to understand and let their hearts be the guide in their selfless service acts, and they seek opportunities to serve and give to others in everything they say or do. Have you ever been impacted by someone who showed you acts of kindness? How did it impact you? How did it change you? Who do you serve?

PART 3

---◆·◆·◆---

GROW YOUR
BUSINESSES

---◆·◆·◆---

*7 Thoughts to Guide you
to Grow Businesses*

1

FOCUS ON FOUNDATION

FOR MOST OF my life my parents owned and operated a small business selling high quality furniture. Prior to owning their own store, my dad managed someone else's furniture store, while my mom upholstered furniture in the basement of our home. My parents started their own business selling and upholstering furniture. Their tagline for their business was "We Service What We Sell!" They knew the importance of serving others, and they made that the core of their business foundation. My parents were known in town as people who could be trusted. They were very good at what they did, and their business flourished for many years. In fact, many other furniture stores opened and closed in our town, but my parents' business made it through some of the most difficult times. They were generous with helping others and the community, and were asked to start teaching upholstering at the local community college in the evenings.

Upholstering is not an easy job. It takes strength and skill to do the type of excellent work that my parents were able to do. They were the best in the business, and they were teaching their skill to other young learners in our local community. The main ingredient separating the good from the great was that they did it right the first time. They put their entire might into it and made sure that the job was done properly and precisely before it went out the door. Their name was on their business, and their name was on the line when it came to their craft. They were known to fix and repair furniture from customers who had bought furniture from them 15 years previously. They held true to their word and serviced what they sold. It was part of their promise.

I had the opportunity to start working at my parents' store when I turned 13. I would go into the store after school or during the summer, where I answered the phones, filed paperwork, dusted furniture, and on occasion would talk with customers who came in if my parents were already talking with other customers. My job was to ask people how I could help them, if there was anything in particular, they were looking for, or if there were any questions they had. I was taught at an early age to treat customers with respect and patience. I watched my parents and older siblings practice giving full attention to the customer and staying attentive and present. More likely than not, at the time of closing of the store or a few minutes prior to that, a customer would come in, sometimes to browse, and other times to buy. It was okay if they wanted to browse, because even if they were just browsing that evening, many times they came back within the month to buy. My parents practiced patience and kindness and knew they were there to serve others and to meet the customers where they needed to be met. A lot of nights that meant staying late in order to meet the customer's needs. Sometimes Mom and Dad would stay at the store, leaving their own agenda behind, and take the time necessary for the customer to choose their furniture. Most, if not all, customers were picking out furniture that was a very large purchase, things that most likely would remain in their homes for many years, even decades. My parents offered custom orders that would sometimes require coordination of color swatches and home interior design expertise. Those decisions could take hours. Their business culture genuinely fostered an environment of excellent customer experience. It was all centered on helping others, and it required the patience and skill to listen to others in order to understand their needs and wants.

Being brought up with entrepreneurial parents taught all seven of us siblings to work hard for what we have. My sister Bonni owns and operates a Marketing and Advertising firm in St. Louis, where her life's work and passion have been poured into her company and the people who work for her company. She has been in the Advertising world since she was a very young woman, and through her tireless grit, powering through all of the obstacles she faced, and her giving heart, she has built her business from the ground up, earning awards as the Top Women Business Owner, Future 50 Awards, Best in Business Award, Best PR Firm Award, and Fastest-Growing Private Companies Award, announced by the St. Louis Business Journal. What I believe is the differentiator is for as many career years as I can remember, a poster hangs on the wall in her office that says, "Stand Up for What is Right Even if You are Standing Alone." I find this to be so meaningful, as it sums up the foundation of what she has built with her business, how she thinks about her clients as well as the people who work for her company. Business foundations are built on character and trust, and it's the people who really make the difference in your business journeys.

As with my parents' furniture business, my sister's business, running any business, or leading a team of people for a company you are employed by, requires a servant leadership mindset. In order to be fully present, you must aim to support the needs of others in the way they need, not necessarily how you want to support them. It is important to ask them what they need, to determine how you can serve them in their context. Doing so creates an environment that fosters great relationships with customers and employees of diverse backgrounds.

Another characteristic I recognized in my parents' business, threaded continuously through my sister's business, is: they were always authentic. They were true to who they are as individuals. I watched my mom work, and she was a force, pure energy, and could work circles around most people. One of her favorite sayings if challenged was "watch me." She was vibrant, engaging, and well-liked by the customers, business partners, and the community. I am grateful that my mom was a businesswoman role model in the way she made a positive impression on me from very young age. My dad was soft-spoken, kind, consistent, persistent, hard-working, tenacious, particular and concise with his craft and honest about doing what he said he would do; his word was and is as good as gold. I learned that serving others comes from the heart, and it shows up in everything we do and say, in our work, in our homes, in our everyday life. While my parents were working, serving others, they were also encouraging and inspiring their kids through their actions. Their working days have long been over, and their impression and foundational business values have been transferred to their children, who are able to express that same passion of serving back to them in their golden years.

As you build your businesses, it is crucial to

set the foundation with all of the attributes that will establish you as a leader with character, trust, and integrity. Know that when you stand up for what is right, even when you are standing alone,

"Business foundations are built on character and trust, and it's the people who really make the difference in your business journeys."

that will make a difference in all of the successes that will follow. What do you stand for? How are you building the foundation of your business?

2

COMMUNICATION WITH CONFIDENCE

BEING ABLE TO connect with people has always been a part of who I am. If you could go back to my elementary school days, you would find that my report cards always said something along the lines of "Robin likes to talk," or, "Robin talks too much," or, "Robin needs to pay more attention in class instead of talking to her classmates." I have been called a social butterfly for the majority of my life, and I am most "alive" when I am surrounded by people of all kinds. I have a passion for learning about people, what means the most to them, how they grew up, who influenced them the most, where they are headed, what is happening in their life right now, and so on. I can genuinely say that I build strong relationships with people of all kinds. I can authentically connect with all walks of life, diversity, anywhere from the homeless person on the street to the CEO in the board-room. I enjoy strong relationships and put my emphasis on the people and not the titles. I naturally gravitated to Business Communication major in both undergrad and graduate level studies. My passion for connecting with people led me to spend the last 2 ½ years continuing to grow myself and honing my skills through a Professional and Executive Coaching program that is accredited by the International Coaching Federation. I have known for years that I need to listen more and talk less, but this program taught me the real importance and the practice of listening to understand.

I come from a very large family. It is common to have three or more conversations going on at once when we are all together; with all members participating in all conversations. It took practice to really start listening more and talking less, but I am so much better off because of it. I still have to reset and remind myself at times that I need to listen and what I have to say isn't always as important as what others are wanting to share with me. I am grateful for the relationships that I have built through the years with my clients, co-workers, friends and family. My passion in life is for the people. When you put people first, your passion shines through, opening doors for extraordinary business results through confident communications between one another.

"When you put people first, your passion shines through, opening doors for extraordinary business results through confident communications between one another."

It allows you to experience meaningful and fulfilling partnerships that can result in phenomenal growth and success.

Are there areas of your communication that you are confident about? Are there areas of communication that you can improve?

3

INNOVATE AND IMPROVE

IN ORDER TO grow businesses, it is imperative to innovate and improve continually. By having a shared vision, perseverance, and tireless grit, you can grow your organization, increase revenue, profit, and reach, impacting the future of the business significantly. Not sharing the vision makes it very difficult to sustain continued growth. Businesses do not just grow automatically, so change is and will always be inevitable. Change brings challenge and opportunity, but growth is not a guarantee. In fact, businesses do not gravitate towards growth; instead, they move toward the mediocre, and then decline. Still, intentional innovation and improvement will lead to prepared growth. But if you do not have an intentional growth plan, the business is unintentionally preparing for decline. There are inhibitors of growth that lead to needless complication, low morale and mindsets, resulting in leaders who are not being developed to continue a growth path that will foster innovation and improvement.

I was 21 years old when I entered the workforce in a corporate environment. In the early 1990's the office scene was a completely different experience from what it is today. The workplace environment allowed chain smokers to smoke at their desks, sexual harassment, rude comments of every kind made toward women, (and I suppose, in some cases, men). Screaming matches between the leaders were daily means of communication. This environment was accepted and expected. I noticed that the young associates modeled that same behavior to fit the mold of what was revered as characteristics of a leader within our corporation in hopes that they too would have the opportunity to fill executive positions. Leadership was white male dominant, and women were trying to make their way into that boardroom. I didn't realize at the time, but this environment was full of unhealthy leadership behaviors that perpetuated unhealthy mindsets and behaviors down the chain of command. I worked as a secretary fulltime and was on the outskirts of management, watching and experiencing the chaos firsthand. Not to make light of the #MeToo movement, but my sister and I often refer to it as #Me2000. We often encountered unwanted advances, without anyone to report them to.

I am grateful for the individuals who encouraged me to move forward with my education, take advantage of the tuition reimbursement, and plow through the necessary steps to continue to grow and evolve, even in that type of crude environment. I didn't know any better, as I was there to make friends, enjoy life and get a paycheck. I began my growth journey back then, taking my first class during my lunch hour, which was English 101. It was the beginning of innovation and improvement of myself. As the years progressed, I began to see a necessary, but moderate, shift in the work environment. Over the last several years, a major innovation in the organization's leadership has drastically improved the way in which we experience the work environment, with only a few remnants of the old environment left.

We know that unhealthy mindsets create unhealthy organizations that hinder their growth. Now that the culture has shifted significantly, there is work underway to mitigate the complexities of the business structure flow, to be dismantled and simultaneously built back, improved and more efficient. Needless confusion often will quietly make its way into a business structure flow, and it will be the very thing that will inhibit or kill growth. The evolution of any business tends toward these complications for reasons such as doubling in size. Since growth will create complexity and complexity will kill growth, I believe the most important aspect in a business structure is for leaders to ensure that needless complexity does not creep into the daily processes and systems.

The workplace culture and leadership dynamic of the 1990s was similar to a broken-down vehicle: it wasn't going to create forward movement until the environment changed or got fixed. As I mentioned earlier, it is the people who make the difference in a business journey, and the potential of the organization rests on the strengths of its leaders. Although difficult at times, it is important to grow the leadership into the new and improved environment.

When teams grow double in size, communication naturally becomes more complicated. For example, someone makes a mistake; a policy is created to address it; a new rule is made because someone is late or isn't adhering to the unwritten rules; or someone overlooks an issue so it is decided that two different departments need to review it. This complicates what used to move quickly and is now a slow and arduous process. Businesses never grow to simplicity. As leaders, our responsibility is to look for anything that slows the pace and anything that complicates the process. In order to innovate and improve the work and environment, work assiduously towards removing unnecessary layers, streamline communication, and build lean effective teams. It is important to empower others and focus on eliminating anything that slows the process. I challenge you to work as hard as you can to

"I challenge you to work as hard as you can to kill a rule, cut a meeting, remove a policy, empower people, and then repeat that process and keep moving."

kill a rule, cut a meeting, remove a policy, empower people, and then repeat that process and keep moving. Watch yourself and your business flourish.

What inefficiencies are hindering your growth? If you want to know your blind spots, ask your team to identify areas that are frustrating or that take too much of their time. What specifically will you work on to simplify immediately? What will you eliminate, reduce, condense, or consolidate?

4

PARTNERSHIPS AND PROGRESSION

I WORK WITH a dynamic team consisting of vibrant and talented executives who have contributed a significant amount of growth to the organization. We call ourselves the "Lucky 7." We have worked collaboratively, and exclusively, with our partnerships to create a growth mindset by planning for opportunity and staying ready for when that opportunity presents itself. Our goal is to capitalize on market opportunities that bring more value to the organization. We know that our mindset will determine our direction and outcomes. We work as a team with a positive outlook on what we are good at, as well as areas that need to be improved so we can be in pursuit of the greatest success we can possibly deliver.

Because we see ourselves as a team via the partnerships we have built with our clients, we are all operating as if we are co-owners of this organization. We understand that if we want to progress and change, we have to change how people think. We have the responsibility to lead our partnerships from a founder's mindset to operate with an obsessive focus on the success of our partnerships and our team. Collectively, the "Lucky 7" believes in limitless horizons and we are on a mission to make history within the organization. We work in an environment of expediential growth, which does not allow for us to become complacent or comfortable, as growth and comfort cannot coexist. Recognizing this adds value to the organization.

We know that we are not where we were when we started this team growth journey, but we are aligned in where we are going and the direction we need to take to get there. As we have been able to experience the growth in our team channel, we as individuals have grown also. As the leader of the "Lucky7" I have made a concerted effort to share the vision and then get out of the way so that the highly competent and talented team I have the pleasure of being a part of can be empowered to lead in every aspect of their roles. As a leader, it is important not to see people merely as a means to get something done but to see getting things accomplished as a tool for developing people. As I mentioned, I empower my team and trust the work and decisions they make for the partnerships they manage. My mission is to empower them and to stay away from undermining their decisions.

Are you giving others you lead permission to fail? Are you giving them the adequate and important feedback to grow? Are you giving them room to rise?

5

ADAPT TO ADVANCE

LIFE AND BUSINESS move at such a fast pace, with changes coming at us so rapidly that technology nearly becomes obsolete before it can be integrated into systems and adopted. People come and go from life and business, and we have to be able to adapt, improvise, and overcome to meet the demands of what is advancing all around us.

What I have learned during the Covid 2020 Pandemic is that the world could stay still, but the work that I was doing was moving at the speed of lightening. While I am no longer jetting off from one place to the next, I wake up daily with a list of priorities, a calendar full of zoom meetings, and an email box that is full of requests and needs from many of my colleagues. Can you relate to this? I am aware that I have adapted to this new way of working out of my home, or living at work, as some people have stated. It has been a time of adapting and adjusting to the communications and needs of the organization. It is a new kind of stress, but I have made the effort to readjust and take advantage of the time that I am home in the evenings and weekends, to pursue my passion to build MyCoachExec. The travel environment I was in earlier wouldn't have allowed me to have the laser focus on setting these goals. Throwing myself into this passion, focusing on my Professional and Personal Growth Journey, has been an outlet for me while I adapted to the "new normal" and improvised on building a plan of launching my business, overcame the fears of the things that were stopping me before, all while managing a very demanding career. Sometimes readjusting means more work to keep focused on the goals we have set for ourselves. As I have reflected, this environment is familiar to me as I have spent the last decade embracing the culture of learning by continuing my education and staying in pursuit of always learning something new. A continual learning path has been a part of how I grow and develop as a person and a leader within the organization.

One of the clients I coached while completing my Professional and Executive Coaching Certification had just gotten out of the military, was adapting to civilian life, and became a mother for the first time, trying to go to school, and work a full-time job. She was experiencing some depression and lack of motivation. She discussed how disciplined she was in the military, how she felt fulfilled and exhilarated with the action of military life. Her new civilian role was taking a toll on her, while in the military she had been operating on a very rigid and intense schedule, in a demanding physical routine and exposed to a dangerous environment nearly every day.

Sometimes when we are thrown into new situations, such as being able to work from home without the added pressure of commuting and travel, or being out of the intense military life experiencing motherhood while working a civilian job, we will have unanticipated reactions. What may appear to some to be the better scenario will bring a different type of stress that comes along with the change. Unless individuals are able to identify and establish a new routine that will drive them forward, they may experience depression or lack of motivation to keep moving forward. It is important to be able to adapt to what life and business throws at us, improvise on the changes, and overcome the obstacles we face to have the kind of success and fulfillment we are seeking, so that we can advance to the next phase of our life and business growth.

How do you feel about your current situation? What do you like about your current environment? How does it suit you to stay as you are?

6

FLOURISH FORWARD

OPPORTUNITIES ARE ABUNDANT in this world, and what you have to do is actively seek them out. The truth is, the biggest difference between successful people and others is that successful people take action. In the difficult experiences I have encountered throughout my life, I've often found myself in waiting mode. I waited for things to change, I waited for approval, I waited until I felt 100% ready, I waited until I had a sign, I waited for others to take action, and so on. What I found out is success does not appear like a package on your front step. It comes with seeking out opportunities, seeking out work, taking risks, trying new paths or new things, falling and getting back up, asking for help or support, and never giving up. Sometimes the hardest step is the first one, but fear of falling is something all of us must come to terms with. In order to have success you cannot allow the fear to become the excuse to keep you from moving forward. I have learned through my experiences that falling can ignite energy that will help you to flourish. As a Professional Executive Coach, I guide my clients to begin a personal and professional growth journey that will lead them to their personal meaning of success. In this process, the journey will create areas where clients will fall or fail, but when we are able to embrace the fear of falling or failing, we are able to continue to stay on the path of intentional growth. My clients have experienced setbacks, disappointments, and low points, but through powerful questions, they find their way back on their charted path, accepting that no one is perfect, and realizing that life and work rarely unfold as planned.

I look back on the path that I have taken and pause for a moment of meditation. I celebrate the times that I took action, stood up for what I believe in, and recognize the learning, growing, and results that were gained because of my willingness to fall forward. I have met many goals along this growth journey, reset, re-established new goals to continue down a path that will encourage, inspire, and challenge others to continue on their own growth journey as well. I have a vision for my business, and I am willing to accept the risk that I will not perfectly get it right. Through experience I know to prepare for the fact that life and work may not unfold the way that I have charted out. However, I am 100% confident that if I do take action, even if things do not go as I plan, I will be on a continued path of learning and growing from the actions, experiences, and opportunities that I have embraced in an effort to continue to flourish forward and leave the legacy I want to leave behind. What are you waiting on or for?

7

PURPOSE AND PASSION

IN BUSINESS AND leadership, we all talk about purpose and passion. Purpose can emerge in different stages of business, but it will be the people who will bring the passion. Have you ever met a business owner or colleague who changes the room dynamic the moment they walk in just because of their energy and magnetism? I grew up in an organization that was founded by an incredible visionary leader. He was an accountant, lawyer, U.S. Navy veteran, an entrepreneur, an extraordinary leader, a father, husband, friend, philanthropist, just to name a few of his titles. He came from a humble upbringing and made his way through serving our country, which afforded him an opportunity to go on to Yale Law School, after his four years of duty in the U.S. Navy. In 1961, he began a business with his co-founder, which is now one of the nation's largest health organizations. This leader impacted our community, many lives, organizations, educational facilities, movements, causes, etc., through his philanthropy foundation, and personal investment. While his legacy is far reaching, for the sake of this book, the focus will be on the legacy he built at his organization.

During the early years of my career, this leader was a part of the daily operations, where I personally was privy to learn from his leadership style just by observing the person he was. He began his business journey in the early 1960s, and many described him as intelligent, charismatic, an entrepreneur, a risk-taker, highly competitive and ambitious. He was social, kind, interested in having conversations with everyone and anyone. He was approachable and gained respect and loyalty from his followers because he made the effort to create genuine encounters with individuals and develop a personal bond. He ate in the lunch room, played wall ball with the associates, asked about your family and remembered the next time he saw you in the elevator, gym, or lunch room. He had charisma, and he inspired all of us to be a part of growing his business. He led by example and had such drive and commitment to the vision of the organization that he created an environment that exuded excitement, creativity, and innovation. He motivated and inspired the associates to overcome any obstacles that were certain to arise in an industry of change. He was able to recognize different strengths and weaknesses in his associates and surrounded himself with intellectual leaders, empowering them to overcome obstacles. This, in turn, stimulated creative solutions, which ignited growth and mobility of vision, even during the years of uncertainty and change.

His legacy still stands today and will always be an example I draw from for inspiration. The organization is thriving and has been through many changes and improvements through the years. My ultimate respect and loyalty remain with the organization that was built on the passion and purpose of his leadership. He was the type of person who, when he walked into a room, his passion and authenticity would ignite energy in all those around him. He worked well into his 70s. Occasionally I saw him walking the halls in the building, years after he had retired, mentoring young executives, or having casual conversations with the associates.

Authentic leadership highlights the importance of a leader's self-awareness and being true to their values. Authentic leaders are well attuned to who they are, what their beliefs and values are, and they do not venture away from them. Their sense of purpose and values guides their actions and the decisions they make. They provide hope, create a bond and relationship with others, exude confidence and have a high standard for ethics. In addition, authentic leaders have a strong moral emphasis, which also exists in service leadership.

The founder's leadership, passion, and shared vision gave purpose to the work we did and still do. Whether he knew it or not, he inspired so many, including me, to invest our time and energy into the company he built because he believed in investing in the people to become better, to give back to others and to our community. I personally will always be grateful for the energy, passion, work ethic, and purpose he had towards his business and its people. My interaction with this leader was not on a daily basis or in a direct business situation, but more as an observer and occasionally having the opportunity to chat with him in the elevator, halls of the workplace, the gym or lobby; but his legacy is clear and there are very few I hold in as high regard as a leader than I do him. I have dedicated many years of my work and life to help continue the passion and purpose set forth by this extraordinary leader.

What is your passion, and what can you grow from it? What would you do if you didn't care about other people's judgment? Imagine you had all the time that you needed to flow into your passion. What steps would you take? If you knew that you could impact hundreds of thousands lives through your business vision, what would stop you from pursuing that vision? What will be your legacy?

FINAL THOUGHTS OF
MY PERSONAL AND PROFESSIONAL
GROWTH JOURNEY

As I CLOSE out my final thoughts on MyCoachExec, Thoughts to Guide You Through Your Personal and Professional Growth Journey, it is important for me to state how grateful I am for all of the experiences I have encountered in my life. I would not be where I am today without those experiences and the people who have come in and gone. I spent my childhood and some of my adult life trying to live up to a standard that was set by a religion that was anything but what it professed: perfection.

The mindset of achieving perfection settled into my thoughts and was a driver of some of my actions. I became extremely sensitive to the reactions of others, pleasing everyone, in hopes that I could be viewed as close to perfect as possible, yet knowing deep down that perfection was not a thing anyone can attain. Through the process of education, my personal coaching sessions, surrounding myself with individuals who support, encourage, inspire, and love me, engulfing myself in my work, and leaning into my spirituality and personal connection to God, I recognize the value I have to share. I now strive to be the best person I can be without the stress of putting energy towards protecting parts of myself and my life that I have spent years trying to ignore or push down. As part of accepting and releasing the areas that cause any negativity or destructive thoughts, I focus on my own personal and professional growth journey and find it more fulfilling than I ever thought possible.

Out of the experiences and opportunities that have come my way, MyCoachExec was born from my true passion for people and the desire to continue to grow myself, others, and businesses. As many of you may know, starting a coaching business is not as easy as you might imagine. It takes a tremendous amount of work, education, and learning about yourself. It is much as I have described in some snapshot moments of my life. It demands that you ask the probing questions: Who am I? Who do I want to serve? What do I offer? It involves trial and error, along with mistakes learned the hard way.

I was uncomfortable when I started to unpack the inner thoughts and experiences I have had. I had previously tried to portray only the good parts of my life, the good side of myself, and it was difficult to emphasize the areas of my life that nearly broke me. However, I recognize that these experiences cannot simply be pushed through without sharing them in some kind of way. They are deep-rooted views;

however, I continue to work on recognizing my critical thoughts in the moment to guide me through my growth journey each day. It has been an amazing journey so far, unpacking all the areas that I had pushed aside, ignored, been ashamed of, held inside of me for so long. The energy I have now from releasing it all is incredibly freeing. Yet it is painful in a few instances, as I have faced up to all of who I am, where I come from, and why I do the things that I do. I realize that MyCoachExec isn't for everyone, but I know it is for some of you. For that, I am grateful. I am proud of thriving through from where I have been, but I am much more excited to get where I am heading. That thought alone gives me a greater vision of who I am today, who I am becoming, and where my personal and professional growth journey will lead me.

MyCoachExec mission is to Encourage, Inspire, and Challenge others to create a path forward through a Personal and Professional Growth Journey, focusing on self, others, and businesses. I know that you will experience the greatest growth journey you have ever experienced if you apply the principles in this book and put the work in to make it happen.

As you begin down your path, you will realize you have an incredible growth journey awaiting you. All you have to do is dream it, craft it, and put it into action. What is your next move?

REFERENCES

Whitmore, J., 2009. Coaching For Performance. 4th ed. London: Nicholas Brealey

Jones, L.B., 1996. The Path Creating Your Mission Statement for Work and for Life

Schuette, K.D., 2009. Soul Purpose: Awaken Your Perfect Self, A Guide to Practical Spirituality

www.businessballs.com/health-and-wellbeing/elisabeth-kubler-ross-five-stages-of-grief

www.worldatlas.com/feature/the-japanese-art-of-kintsugi

Kool and the Gang – Celebration

Kondo, M., 2016. Spark Joy, an illustrated master class on the art of organizing and tidying up

Lightning Source UK Ltd.
Milton Keynes UK
UKHW021300270721
387818UK00006B/433/J